William Binney

Proceedings of the City Council of Providence on the Death of Abraham Lincoln,

with the oration delivered before the municipal authorities and citizens

June 1, 1865. Vol. 1

William Binney

Proceedings of the City Council of Providence on the Death of Abraham Lincoln, *with the oration delivered before the municipal authorities and citizens June 1, 1865. Vol. 1*

ISBN/EAN: 9783337301316

Printed in Europe, USA, Canada, Australia, Japan

Cover: Foto ©ninafisch / pixelio.de

More available books at **www.hansebooks.com**

PROCEEDINGS

OF THE CITY COUNCIL OF PROVIDENCE

ON THE DEATH OF

ABRAHAM LINCOLN:

WITH THE

ORATION

DELIVERED BEFORE THE MUNICIPAL AUTHORITIES AND CITIZENS,
JUNE 1, 1865,

BY WILLIAM BINNEY, Esq.

PROVIDENCE:
KNOWLES, ANTHONY & CO., PRINTERS.
1865.

PROCEEDINGS OF THE CITY COUNCIL.

A BRAHAM LINCOLN, President of the United States, died in the city of Washington, on the 15th day of April, 1865, by the foul hand of assassination. The telegraph, which had been flashing the joyful news of victory and the fall of the rebellion, carried the tidings throughout the land. Deep sorrow filled all hearts which had learned to respect and then love the pure patriot who had gone.

The Mayor of the City of Providence called a special meeting of the City Council, on the 17th of April, and delivered the following message :—

MESSAGE OF THE MAYOR.

MAYOR'S OFFICE,
Providence, April 17th, 1865.

GENTLEMEN OF THE CITY COUNCIL :—

I have convened you, at this time, to take such action as you may deem expedient, in reference to the great calamity that has just fallen upon our nation. The President of the United States has come to his death by the hands of an assassin. History affords no parallel to this atrocious crime.

Abraham Lincoln, called for the second term, by the free voice of the people, to be the guide of the nation's destiny, while unceasingly devoting his term of service to its welfare, and knowing no policy, save that which should best secure its prosperity,—exercising the powers of government at his command, solely for the restoration of the national authority,—ever tempering justice with much mercy,—has fallen a victim to the power that he was seeking to overcome with love.

The events of the past week have given rise to the feeling, that although the dawn of peace seemed breaking and the dark clouds of war seemed rolling away, yet our nation was really in greater danger than at any previous time. The liberal terms granted, upon its surrender, to the army under the command of the second of arch traitors ; the indications that were being manifested of a magnanimous treatment of men, guilty of the blackest of crimes ; the feeling of generosity that was being cultivated among the people of the North, towards the men who had not only raised their hand against the government, but who also visited upon its captured soldiers a line of treatment unparalleled in the history of civilized warfare ;—these were greater dangers than any we have yet encountered, and they are only checked by a crime, whose baseness will astound the world, and which clearly signifies that the power which has instigated and carried on this wicked rebellion is capable of any barbarity which will aid its infamous designs.

That Divine Providence, which through these years of trial has strengthened and protected our President, upon which he leaned with confidence and submission, and to which he looked at all times for consolation and support, has, at the very hour of his triumph, permitted his removal, and granted to him, as to the Patriarch of old, only a distant view of the promised land.

Let us, in this hour of bereavement, trust in that same Providence, to guide us safely on as a nation, and to grant unto us that the successor of him who hath been so suddenly removed may be armed with power and might to drive our enemies out from among us, and by a strong and vigorous policy, teach the world and the generations yet to come, that treason against such a government as ours is not to be rewarded with honor or magnanimity.

Since the death of the first President of the United States, no man has passed away whose death has called forth such general expressions of sorrow, and such universal lamentations, as that of Abraham Lincoln. His honesty of purpose, his integrity of character, his simplicity of heart, all endeared him to the nation; and the spontaneous bursts of grief from the stoutest hearts are the evidences of the love and veneration in which the loyal people held their chosen ruler. That one so kind and gentle in his disposition should have died by the hand of the murderer, a victim to the power of darkness, has stirred the feelings of our citizens as they were never moved before.

Wednesday, the 19th instant, being the day designated for the funeral of the venerated dead, I recommend that it be set apart as a day of public mourning, and that a Committee of your body be authorized to make arrangements for suitable services on the occasion.

THOMAS A. DOYLE, MAYOR.

REMARKS OF WILLIAM BINNEY, ESQ.,

PRESIDENT OF THE COMMON COUNCIL.

MR. PRESIDENT:—

There are occasions in life when the human tongue, however eloquent, has an opportunity to learn its utter feebleness. There are griefs of which the only palliatives are silence and reflection. There are crises in the life of the nation, when the soul of every man, prostrated by the perception of gloom on every hand, turns in upon itself, and is paralyzed by the consciousness of an equal sympathetic gloom within; and when feeling, with the force of an instinct, bids us to commune with ourselves and be still. I need not say, Sir, that this is such an occasion; and did I listen to my own desires, no word of mine should intrude between the thoughts of any in this assembly, and their own convictions of our terrible calamity. But, Sir,

I do not forget that the privileges which are allowed to individuals must be abandoned, when, however humble, they stand as representatives of the community in which they live; or that propriety and decency demand that the spontaneous sorrow of the members should have an opportunity to crystalize itself into the more formal grief of the body politic. It is for this reason, and because this Council is the formal representative of the citizens of Providence, that I address you these few words.

Before the fatal year of 1861 had dawned upon this country, the present generation of men had known but few such epochs as those to which I have alluded; but in the four long years which since then have passed over our land,—at times irradiating it with the full brilliancy of sunlight, and at times covering it with a thick impenetrable cloud,—your own memory will suggest but too many instances. I need but recall the bewilderment which brooded on every face when the news of our first great defeat fell on us like a thunder-bolt from the clear sky; or to that day when we learned slowly and by fragments that all the struggles of the Peninsula, its bloody battles, its weary marches, its patient watchings, the unyielding faith of its heroic army, were as yet all in vain; and that the host which had listened to the bells of Richmond as they beleaguered it, now beaten and crushed back, could send us no brighter bulletin than temporary safety on the banks of the James. I could point you to that day, when, with beating hearts, we almost counted the footsteps of an insolent enemy marching on to our very capital, and when we scarcely dared to breathe, until Antietam gave us courage. I could point you to that cloud which, rising behind the Wilderness and Chancellorsville, swept northward until it burst upon the hillside of Gettysburg, and though it burst in blood upon that consecrated spot, yet there, rolled back its torn and emptied bulk and came no farther. But, Sir, be your memory, never so retentive of the vicissitudes of these slow rolling years, I feel that you will agree with me that in all their sorrowful record they can show us no such day as the fifteenth day of April 1865. Then, for the first time, the nation began to see the dawning of an abiding peace. Victory after victory had gladdened our ears. The chief army of the rebellion was captive to that army which had so long watched and fought it. Bonfires and torches all over the land gave expression to the general hilarity ; when, in an instant, upon the stillness of that tranquil morning, the appalling news crashed over us, that our President had been assassinated—that that great and good man, that man dear to our hearts beyond all other men, that man precious to the nation beyond all other men, was rapidly dying, if not dead, and this, too, at the hands of a rebel assassin. Sir, he is dead, and it is around his mangled but peaceful remains that the nation is pouring out unpurchasable tears. In the presence of such a mysterious and such an immeasurable calamity, it cannot be expected that we should rightly appreciate what it is that we have lost. This is not the time, nor are mine the lips, to tell what that man was to this nation, much less to utter any conjecture of what, in the Providence of God, he might have been. If we desire his portrait we can find it shrined in the grateful hearts of millions of freemen, both white and black, all over this land. If we desire to know what he has done, we can look around. Look not only here to this community, whose soil was never tainted by the foot of an armed rebel, and where peaceful industry has been permitted to create its blessings in unexpected plenty, but look over our continent : we can behold that majestic river of the West again offering its broad bosom as the highway for a nation of freemen : we can see enfranchised Maryland, liberated Louisiana, free Missouri, the Atlantic seaboard opened to a peaceful commerce from one end of our domain to the other : we can see a purged Constitution ; Slavery transformed from a hideous fact into a ghastly but harmless memory ; a disintegrated Confederacy ; its Congress fugitives, its arch traitor a vagabond in the land ; or again we can behold the flood of love pouring from a grateful nation toward that man, and swelling back to every human being in it from the fullness of his own great heart. And if we will venture into the future, we may behold that sagacious, kindly nature, harmonizing, arranging, re-adjusting a restored government, and then administering it, in the principles of obedience to God and love to man. Then, sir, if we have the heart to do it, we can turn and look upon that silent corpse. It seems to me, Mr. President, that the humblest man in the nation may feel what the most eloquent never can express.

I have said already too much, or too little. I have the honor to offer for the adoption of this Council the resolutions which I hold in my hand, and which, with the permission of the chair, I will read.

Mr. Binney offered the following resolutions, which were unanimously adopted by both boards of the City Council :—

RESOLUTIONS OF THE CITY COUNCIL OF THE CITY OF PROVIDENCE,

PASSED APRIL 17, 1865.

WHEREAS, Under every dispensation of an All Wise and Merciful God, the only attitude for a Christian people is that of truthful submission,

Resolved, That we, the City Council of the City of Providence, representing a loyal and a Christian community, do bow our hearts before Almighty God, under the crushing blow which he has permitted us to receive, and that we humbly implore Him who maketh rulers, and unmaketh them at His will, to be henceforth in an especial manner, the Ruler, Guide and Governor of our sorrow stricken land.

Resolved, That in the death of the late President of the United States, at this crisis of their destiny, we endure the culminating calamity of our nation. In his murder, we behold the crowning infamy of our age. Yet, " though perplexed we are not in despair ; though cast down we are not destroyed ; and over his yet unburied body, we renew our allegiance to the great cause for which he lived, and pledge a deathless opposition to the rebellion at whose felon hand, he died.

Resolved, That so long as patriotism shall be accounted a virtue ; so long as untarnished honesty, unflinching courage, a life-long devotion to duty, and the sacrifice of life in its defense, can wake an echo in the soul ; while a thoughtful and sagacious intellect can claim the admiration of man, or a blameless life challenge his respect ; while firmness that reverses cannot shake, nor slander dissolve, shall merit his praise, or the consciousness of benefits confessed awaken his gratitude and love ; so long shall the name and memory of Abraham Lincoln be consecrated in the hearts and history of this preserved and grateful nation.

Resolved, That in this awful crime at which humanity stands aghast, we see the familiar features of that rebellion whose hell-given energies have so long desolated our land. It was not enough to delude the nation with the sophistries of perverted intellect, to corrupt it with the poison of a baneful example, to insult it with the arrogance of a more than Pagan barbarism. It has demanded the nation's life, and has wielded the sword, the torch, and the dagger, with undiscriminating and congenial joy. Surging forth upon a peaceful land, with Slavery as its new Gospel of conquest, it has, for four long years, defied the clemency of God and the authority of human law. Unnumbered battle-fields retain the victims of its open warfare ; the bones of sixty thousand of our brethren starved in its prisons, attest the infamy of its secret decrees ; the midnight ocean has grown lurid with the flames of its piracies ; and now, in the hour of its prostration, when the Majesty of the Republic had well nigh crushed its organized strength, the most precious life of our people has gone out before the pistol of its assassins. An outraged nation must henceforth regard the friends of *such* a rebellion as the enemies of the human race.

Resolved, That we tender to the afflicted widow and family of our late President, our most earnest and heartfelt sympathy in this their terrible calamity. Bereaved for the nation, they should be, and we feel that henceforth they are, the Nation's care.

Resolved, That for him who is now the President of the United States, and upon whom this darkest villany of rebellion has

2

laid the responsibility and duty of its complete extinction, we invoke the protection and the blessing of God, and the loyalty and confidence of our fellow-countrymen. May his mind be enlightened, his courage sustained, his hand strengthened, and his efforts directed and prospered in the great work before him ; until, in the full success of a stable peace, a united nation, and a vanquished and extirpated treason, he and the whole people may live to enjoy that great blessing for which the loved and lamented Lincoln prayed and toiled and died.

Resolved, That His Honor the Mayor be, and he is hereby, requested to transmit a copy of the resolutions just passed to the President of the United States, asking him to communicate the same to the family of the deceased.

Mr. Coggeshall offered the following resolutions, which were also adopted :—

RESOLUTIONS APPOINTING A COMMITTEE OF ARRANGEMENTS.

Resolved, That Messrs. Metcalf, Coggeshall, Gladding, Whitaker, Parkhurst, Robbins and Thomas, with Aldermen Jones and Lester, be appointed a committee to make such arrangements as may seem to them advisable in commemoration of the sad event that has fallen upon this nation.

Resolved, That said committee be authorized to draw on the City Treasurer for such sum of money as may be required to defray the expenses of a proper expression of the love and respect which this community bear to the memory of the late President of the United States.

Under and pursuant to the aforegoing resolutions, the Committee of Arrangements issued the following notice :—

MUNICIPAL OBSERVANCE OF THE PRESIDENT'S DAY OF MOURNING.

The following arrangements have been made for the observance of Thursday, June 1st, by the City Government, through the Committee appointed for that purpose.

A procession will be formed from the Council Chamber, under the direction of the City Marshal, at 3½ o'clock, P. M., in the following order :—

Detachment of Police.
Band.
Committee of Arrangements.
Orator of the Day and Officiating Clergymen.
City Marshal.
His Honor the Mayor and Board of Aldermen.
Members of the Common Council.
City Clerk and Clerk of the Common Council.
City Officers.
His Excellency the Governor and Staff.
Militia Officers, General, Regimental, Line and Staff.
His Honor the Lieutenant Governor and Secretary of State.
Attorney General, State Auditor and General Treasurer.
United States Senators and Representatives.
Officers of the United States Army and Navy.
Retired Officers of the United States Army and Navy.
Judges of State Courts and Clerks.
District Judge, Attorney, Clerk and Marshal.
Officers of the Customs and Post Office Department.
Members of the State Legislature.
Ex-Governors.
Ex-Mayors.
Members elect of the City Government.
Members of the School Committee.

Superintendent of Public Schools, and Grammar Masters.
Clergymen of the City and vicinity.
President and Officers of Brown University.
President and Officers of all Civic Bodies.

The procession will march to the Beneficent Congregational Church, on Broad street, where an Oration will be delivered by the Hon. William Binney, and appropriate services will be held, commencing at 4 o'clock.

Persons intending to join the procession will meet at the Council Chamber at 3 o'clock p. m.

ORDER OF SERVICES

ON THE DAY APPOINTED BY THE PRESIDENT OF THE UNITED STATES AS A DAY OF HUMILIATION AND MOURNING FOR THE DEATH OF ABRAHAM LINCOLN, LATE PRESIDENT OF THE UNITED STATES; HELD IN THE BENEFICENT CONGREGATIONAL CHURCH, BEFORE THE CITY GOVERNMENT AND CITIZENS OF THE CITY OF PROVIDENCE, THURSDAY, JUNE 1, 1865.

E. A. KELLEY, Organist and Music Director.

1. Voluntary on the Organ. FUNERAL MARCH. *Battiste.*

2. Chorus. COLUMBIA MOURNS. . . . . *Neukomm.*

Columbia, mourn! His course is o'er; the brave, the mighty is no more! Mourn, Columbia! let all your streams of sorrow flow. We have sinned; we fell; we scorned our God! He died beneath the assassin's rod. O day of bitterness! O day of woe! Mourn, Columbia! Mourn!

3. Reading the Scriptures.

4. Quartette. . . . . *Spohr.*

Blest are the departed who in the Lord are sleeping.

5. Prayer.

6. Chorus for men's voices. "INTEGER VITÆ." *Fleming,*

" He who is upright, kind, and free from errors,
Seeks not the aid of men to guard him;
Calmly he moves, untouched by guilty terrors,
    Strong in his virtues.

" Tranquil and peaceful is his path to heaven,
Where, in the brightness of the Saviour's presence,
Souls of the martyrs, purified by suff'ring,
    Wait to receive him.

" Leader and martyr, fallen in his armor!
Lives yet our Captain, strong is our salvation,
Fails not our victory, dies not the nation,—
    Christ our deliv'rer."

7. Oration, by WILLIAM BINNEY, Esq.

8. Chorus. "I HEARD A VOICE." . . . *E. A. Kelley.*

"I heard a voice from heaven, saying unto me, Write, from henceforth blessed are the dead who die in the Lord, for they rest from their labors, and their works do follow them."

9. Concluding Prayer.

10. Hymn, by O. W. HOLMES.

Music.—OLD HUNDRED.

O Lord of Hosts! Almighty King!
Behold the sacrifice we bring!
To every arm Thy strength impart,
Thy Spirit shed through every heart.

Wake in our breasts the living fires,
The holy faith that warmed our sires:
Thy hand hath made our nation free ;
To die for her is serving Thee.

God of all Nations! Sovereign Lord!
In Thy dread name we draw the sword,
We lift the starry flag on high,
That fills with light our stormy sky.

No more its flaming emblems wave
To bar from hope the trembling slave;
No more its radiant glories shine
To blast with woe a child of Thine.

From treason's rent, from murder's stain,
Guard Thou its folds till Peace shall reign,—
Till fort and field, till shore and sea,
Join our loud anthem, PRAISE TO THEE!

11. Benediction.

ORATION.

ORATION.

My Fellow Citizens :—

WHEN a human life is transferred from this world, how seldom do we apprehend what has been done. Revelation assures us that for one immortal being, a catastrophe has been reached, more portentous than the dissolution of a world. Instinct and reason assent to the truth. Some momentary palpitations warn us of its import for ourselves, but the influence is feeble and evanescent. Here and there in retired spots, there is a pause. In isolated homes, there are a few sorrowing hearts. A few eyes drop bitter tears, a few prayers press up to God from the depths of a heaving breast, a corpse remains to be reverently committed to the earth, and the minister of God repeats his words of warning or of resignation. But the great aggregate of humanity advances in its solemn progress, scarcely conscious that an atom has been withdrawn from its bulk. The numberless activities of man are unrestrained. Ambition glows with unslackened fire, toil struggles with the same anxiety, science explores with undiverted attention, thought and fancy soar with unrestricted sweep, and the very mourners make haste to resume their places in the moving throng.

3

That majestic ocean current which borders our land moves ever on its destined course. From all sides, it is dissolving into the cold abyss which environs it, but the lightnings flash about it, the vapor exhales from it, and it presses onward tempering a continent, its energies the unconscious ministers of the Almighty's love.

To the law which controls its movement there is no interruption, but that which humanity obeys is happily more yielding. Hence it is, that when the life with which we part has been conspicuous above its fellows, from whatever cause ; when the lustre of position, the splendor of talent, the radiance of virtue, or the glare of wealth, has fixed the eyes of men upon some unit of their number, we do for a moment stop. We turn our gaze from what is, to what has been ; and consent to ask of death, what life is. Yet the pause, at most, is brief.

But should there come a time when millions swell the note of lamentation, and the sun sets and rises again upon an unsubsided sorrow ; should we perceive the ordinary pursuits of a nation suspended, its usual interests laid aside, its common topics abjured ; and did we hear the throbbing of unnumbered hearts in the solemn unison of grief, we might feel assured that we then beheld humanity in the rarest and most majestic of its attitudes.

Such a spectacle the American nation has but recently exhibited. If the deepest melancholy has surrounded it, it has yet been full of a gracious benediction. Like all great blessings, it has been purchased with a sacrifice, and the price we have paid for it has been our choicest and our best. The fullness and the value of the cost must remain for the future to disclose, but faith already invites us to regard it as the source of deep and lasting good. It is because we acknowledge its magnitude, and would learn what we may of its significance, that we are assembled here to-day. The President of the United States has summoned the nation to reflect upon its loss. The authorities of our city have responded to his request, and have appointed me to address you upon the solemn topic, and it is their wish which I obey.

You have buried a murdered President. Your voices have swelled the mighty chorus of sorrow, which rose from the bosom of this continent. Every token of sympathy and grief, which outward act, or spoken word, or chastened thought, could render, has been shown by you. Every pulpit has grown eloquent upon the unparalleled theme. The press, all over the land, has become the mouth-piece of the universal anguish. Private associations, the fraternities of trade and commerce, municipal and State governments, have made haste to offer their appreciative tributes to the dead, and to renew their allegiance to the living. A mournful procession has wound its slow course to the West, waking in hamlet and city the same touching response, and now the sacred remains which it carried with it rest in the soil of their western home. The pulses of life have resumed their ordinary beat. The interests of the living again occupy our thoughts. The future. with its expectations, anxieties and doubts, beckons us away from the past. The first fervor of your emotions has unavoidably subsided, but you refuse to part company with your grief, until it shall have yielded you its blessing.

I am to speak to you of the life and character and death of Abraham Lincoln. But as I take that name upon my lips, how sensibly must I feel my incapacity.

There are themes so rich that their affluence is oppressive. There are occasions so grand that they dwarf our powers and paralyze our energies. There are characters which dwell outside of description, because their expanse out-measures apprehension. If this be true, I appeal to you, if it was ever more so than now, and in reference to the present subject. If I can conceive of any qualities capable of doing justice to that subject, they would be those of the lamented dead. His keen sagacity, his ripened wisdom, his singleness of purpose, his manly sense, his firm and living faith, his all embracing charity,—these might approach the task nor dread discomfiture. They are unfortunately incommunicable. Their results are our legacy if we will accept it, but the qualities themselves are graces which man wins by conflict; he can never receive them as a gift.

One gift, however, the illustrious dead was able to confer upon the race, a rich and pregnant gift, holding in its grasp a thousand others scarce inferior to itself. It is the spirit of his life. Plain, unvarying, easily apprehended, stretching like a luminous thread through the line of his years, it gleams before us as obedience to the duty of the hour; obedience unsolicitous of results, and asking of duty nothing but her Heaven signed credentials. That spirit I invoke for all; I invoke it for myself.

When a people is creating history, it seldom has a desire to transcribe it, or the leisure and capacity to read its current record aright. The physical and intellectual activities which such periods evoke, have a re-active influence upon each other, which tends constantly to exaggeration. The ordinary and verified standards of feeling and judgment are overthrown.

Events and men move before the eye in a confused
whirl, where distinct vision is impossible. Small things
from their nearness or the grotesqueness of their position
seem great, while the great are too near to be fully
embraced. Passions and prejudices, anxieties, hopes
and fears, roll about us on all sides their volumes of
mist. No height discloses itself from whose tranquil
summit we can survey the panorama of commotion, nor
could we ascend it, were it there. We are ourselves a
part of the scene. History and her handmaid, biogra-
phy, demand a more quiet period, and a point of greater
distance, before they can commence their necessary
work. All that can be produced at times like these is
such an outline sketch as may gratify curiosity, or impart a form to our vague conceptions. It will be the
task of a day remote from this, to portray the magnificent movement of destiny in this western world, and to
paint the master spirit who linked himself to that destiny beyond all other men, because he bound himself to
the eternal principles from which it was evolved. The
duty of the present hour will be fulfilled, if I shall be
able to place before you such a fragmentary outline as,
while it gives no portrait of the man or time, lets something of the grandeur of the one, of the goodness and
greatness of the other, and of the relation between the
two, shine through the gaps.

ABRAHAM LINCOLN was born in what is now La-Rue
county, Kentucky, on the 12th day of February, 1809,
and in that comparative wilderness of a half-century
ago, he passed the first six or seven years of his life.
His parents were Virginians, of whom we know little
more than their integrity and industry. Frontier life,
in that day, was something which required and devel-

oped the sturdier virtues, but it made small demand, as it gave but little scope, for the refinements of culture and taste. Thomas Lincoln, the father, was illiterate and poor. The labor of his hands was his support. Yet a sense of his own deficiencies sharpened the desire to educate his son, and his affection was at all times active in procuring for the boy such books and schooling as his own scanty means and the primitive neighborhood allowed. The mother was a religious woman, one of those to whom the Bible is a real and living thing ; who make it a friend and guide, and who feel that all has been done for a child when his eyes and heart have been opened to its pages. At her side he learned to read the sacred volume, and throughout his trying and eventful life it is believed to have been ever at his own.

Satisfied by experience that residence in a slave State was disastrous to one whose only capital was his labor, the father decided in 1816 to abandon this Kentucky home, which slavery degraded, and seek a new one on the free soil of Indiana, then about to be admitted into the Union.

The spot selected was among the picturesque river bluffs of the Ohio. A clearing was soon made, a log-hut erected, and this was the home of Lincoln until 1830. Thirteen years, eventful enough to him and to us, though unmarked by outward signs of their significance, were passed in this cabin. It is easy to picture to ourselves that simple home. There was abundance of work for those young hands in subduing an untamed nature. There were hardship and exposure in many forms to strengthen his bodily frame, and toughen his courage and endurance. If the intercourse and advan-

tages of more developed civilization were wanting, so
also were its allurements and dissipations. Earnestness,
sobriety and honest toil spread a pure and invigorating
atmosphere about the spot. There were the evenings
for such study as was in his power, and for the
thoughts and reflection to which it might give rise.
Books, of course, were few, but they were not wholly
absent, and such as he procured would seem to have
had a singular fitness for his mental and moral growth.
In 1831, a new emigration conducted the family to
the central part of Illinois. Again the son's labor is
given to build the house and fence the farm. But the
time had come for him to leave the paternal roof and
try the world for himself. A vigorous and hardy frame,
a courageous and truthful soul, a clear and strong intelligence, a hopeful spirit and a simple but steady faith
in God and the right, were his outfit; and it must be
confessed neither scanty nor ill-assorted. Of the world
outside he knew but little ; of that within himself, he
had learned what such a life alone could teach.

From this time until 1837, when we find him prac-
tising law in Springfield, Illinois, he tried most of the
phases of western life, always earnestly, and usually
with success. Farm laborer, clerk, storekeeper, county
surveyor, postmaster and member of the Legislature,
each in its turn, and all the while studying diligently
at the law, which he had chosen for his ultimate profes-
sion, he omitted no opportunity for self-support or
usefulness; and that some coloring of military life
might not be wanting, he served with fidelity and merit
as Captain of volunteers in the Indian war of 1832.

Until 1858, Mr. Lincoln continued to practice law,
with a growing reputation for ability, and to attract the

regard of his fellow citizens, who selected him to repre-
sent them in the Congress of 1847.

But it was in 1858, that what had thus far been a
local reputation expanded into a national one; and
that the great Republican party of the free States began
to look to Mr. Lincoln as among the ablest and most
earnest of its leaders.

Viewed merely by himself at this time, he presents
a striking figure. Tall and vigorous in body, and with a
mind quite as healthful, there was neither elegance nor
grace in either. The society in which he moved did
not exact, and had not developed them. His virtues
and intelligence were distinctively American. His
training had been equally so, and he was the natural
product of the two. It was not the figure of a hero,
or which fancy could hope to develop into the heroic.
But it was the figure of a man, to be respected, to
be loved, to be trusted; of a strong, truthful, genial,
quick-witted man, a reliable and powerful friend, a dangerous but fair antagonist. Thought and action alike
betokened in him unused and undeveloped strength.
But it seems to me that we shall fail to see him in his
true proportions, if we overlook the remarkable background from which he stood relieved. Let me attempt
briefly to sketch that background, as it appears to me.

The curious naturalist who follows the trail of our
western emigration, is often struck by the presence of
weeds along the track, for which he finds it difficult to
account. They are not indigenous to the soil, nor are
they found except where the foot of the foreigner has
been. No conscious hand has sown them. They are
the growth of those unconsidered seeds, which were
native to the stranger's home. They have clung to

him unperceived through his ocean voyage. and equally
unconsciously are scattered about his new abode. The
seminal principles of that outgrowth of thought and
feeling which we call civilization propagate themselves
as spontaneously, and still more widely, than the germs
of vegetable life. Less various perhaps, they are more
constant to their type, and philosophy works backward
from their presence to their origin, with a confidence
that is seldom misplaced.

In the year 1620, two vessels dropped their anchors
in waters which are already emblematic, and must remain so to the American eye, through all time. Both
voyages were projected in the same foreign land, and
may be fairly said to have represented the conflicting
characteristics of the same people. Dutch piety and
love of freedom bade God-speed to the men who landed
by the Massachusetts Bay, with liberty and law in their
hands. Dutch enterprise and love of wealth sent their
cargo of slaves to the banks of the James. Unnumbered and unnoticed seeds of good and evil came with
both. The life of each began at once to beget new life,
and as their forms drew near to each other, and the
border land between the two began to fill, reciprocal
action commenced and a hybrid growth sprung up.
Two forms of civilization, one where capital and labor
were bound by an equal and beneficial alliance, and the
other where labor was the property and bond slave of
capital, had each selected its domain in a new and pro-
lific world, and thenceforth they grew together, auxili-
aries in noble works, in works of imperishable benefit,
but radical, though immature, antagonists.

During our Colonial life, and especially in the condi-
tion of public sentiment, not only in the mother country,

4

but throughout the world, this essential antagonism was almost unperceived. But it was there none the less, and none the less essential. When the fetters of colonial subjection were first broken, the conflict began. Liberty sent forth her noble protest, in the Declaration of Independence, but slavery had already tampered with the language in which it was expressed. But when the removal of all foreign control left the nation to the influences of her own systems, it assumed its real position. The great territorial ordinance would have been its death blow, but it turned aside the stroke. The constitution might have destroyed it, but it moulded the constitution to its ends. Working gradually, but working steadily, it created the fugitive slave clause, and forged that chain in which so many of freedom's giants have writhed in vain. Under the constitution its struggles have been powerful and unintermitted, and in early opposing Congressional interference with the territories not included in the ordinance of 1787, it prepared the ground for all its future triumphs. It was combatted steadily, but it grew. Circumstances favored it beyond anticipation. The slave trade in the appointed time had become illegal ; moral and religious sentiment was glowing, a dreadful perception of its inherent wrong began to grow even in its midst; but alongside, and ready for the use, were allies destined to more than counterbalance their combined force. The cotton plant waved its pods prophetic of future wealth. The genius of Whitney became the property of the world, and lent its vital aid. The vast territory of Louisiana was ceded to the Union, and stretched out its arms to both. A rich expanse lay before it, and it made haste to enter. The constitution was ignored, that blessings for which it provided no channel might swell in upon the land, with a golden irrigation. A new departure was taken, a different voyage commenced; and Slavery sprang gaily and defiantly to the helm. The progress thence was rapid and fatal. Farewell now to apologetic defense. Slave trading, slave breeding became the policy, because they seemed the necessity of the time. Slavery was no longer with the South an evil to be tolerated ; it was a right to be sustained. The intellect of the South trained itself for the work. The armories of the past and present were ransacked for weapons of protection or assault. The chimera of secession, fostered into new vigor and bulk, planted its horrid form before the sacred institution, and forbade approach. The religion of Christ and the creed of popular sovereignty were alike bid to speak in its behalf. The destinies of free millions were as nothing to it. The legislature of the only great Republic of the world was but its tool. The elements were unchained, and the indifference, the passions, the tremors and the aspirations of a great race heaved in unorganized tumult. The freeman felt that his birthright was in danger. The slaveholder felt his power and grew furious in its use ; and all around stood the timid virtues, hoping all things, believing all things, daring nothing. There was a party rising in the land a million strong. It had a prescience, a courage, a purpose, which were its strength ; but it needed a man. This was the background as I view it, against which, in 1858, Mr. Lincoln stood forth on the prairie land of Illinois.

The contest which he entered was for a Senatorship, the antagonist was Stephen A. Douglas, the audience was the freemen of the West of every shade of opinion ;

but the battle and the victory were for human freedom, and for all coming time, and nobly did he open the immortal tournament. Listen to his words in the first of those speeches which convulsed Illinois in the summer and autumn of 1858. Truly, the trumpet gave no uncertain sound. " If we could first know where we are, and whither we are tending, we could better judge what to do, and how to do it. We are now far in the fifth year since a policy was initiated with the avowed object and confident promise of putting an end to slavery agitation. Under the operation of that policy, that agitation has not only not ceased, but has constantly augmented. In my opinion it will not cease, until a crisis has been reached and passed. 'A house divided against itself cannot stand.' I believe this government cannot endure permanently, half slave and half free. I do not expect the Union to be dissolved. I do not expect the house to fall, but I do expect, it will cease to be divided. It will become all one thing or all the other." Words remarkable enough in prediction, but how much more so in their result.

Here, we cannot but observe, was no announcement of a policy. There was not even an expression of a wish. A plain statement of that indwelling faith which is so often unconscious prophecy—that was all. From a foremost man of a young and vigorous party we might have looked for something different. A party Shibboleth, a code of tactics, an appeal to passion, or to prejudice ; a battle cry ; these are what we might have expected, but there came only a temperate but far reaching declaration of belief. Only a few years have passed, and it is the demonstrated creed of a race.

At that time, if there was anything chiefly needed, it was a faith such as this. A faith not in policies, not in expediencies, not in plans, or compromises, or hostilities as such ; but in essential truths. It was Mr. Lincoln's great advantage that he possessed it. It was his great power that he was always possessed by it. Throughout all that vigorous and animated struggle, contending against an antagonist of undisputed force and great popularity, and one well skilled to use every faculty of a vigorous mind, a robust body, an iron will, a voice of rare compass and expression, and a nature of noble and attractive traits, in swaying the judgments, the feelings, and the sympathies of men ; this uncouth but still attractive western lawyer, held that faith on high, and conquered in its sign. The immediate prize, it is true, was lost ; Mr. Douglas was again elected Senator ; but the people understood Mr. Lincoln, and his destiny was fixed.

If we follow the course of that debate and of the speeches auxiliary to it, we shall be forced to confess that faith was far from being his only power, though it gave momentum to the rest. Every one of them exhibits a man whose conception of ideas was clear, defined and comprehensive ; his perception of things distinct, and of relations, remarkably so ; his logic thorough and connected, though not concise ; his memory retentive of analogies ; his language plain, but vigorous, apt, descriptive and copious ; his fancy alive, but never in excited action ; his wit homely, but bright and pointed. All these faculties he used easily, and effectively, holding the sympathies by an unruffled bearing, a genial temper, a courageous port, and by the mysterious emanations of a truth loving, truth speaking, truth seeking soul. Ithuriel's spear could not have more clearly revealed the sophistry concealed in popular sovereignty, than did his pointed sentences. The nicest analysis of science could not expose more surely than his lips, the essential contrast of slavery the matter of indifference, with slavery the moral, social and political wrong. He acknowledged the necessity of parties, and, therefore, was a party man. He accepted a party platform because he approved it, while he was slow to commit himself to its modes of action. He understood the constitution of his country, and gave it an unreserved obedience. To the State rights and State obligations which it guarantied, he adhered. His line of policy towards the slave question was not clear, nor was it, perhaps, so far stretching as that of his party ; but his vision of the future and his estimate of the thing, were surpassed in none. There was room for growth, and capacity as well. And the growth in due time came.

This man, such as I have endeavored to sketch him, became, in 1861, the duly elected President of the United States ; and history will record that he was so announced to the assembled Senate and House of Representatives, by Vice-President Breckinridge, his rival at the time, his assassin since.

Since that announcement, four awful years have swept over the land. They have carried to the dusky past, their swollen record of crime and virtue. Thick thronging incidents of victory and defeat, of apostacy and faith, of cruelty and charity, of dismay and exultation, have burdened the memory almost beyond its power ; and overtaxed emotion in vain endeavors to renew its earlier agitations. Still the time is not yet

too distant for us to recall something of that gloom, in
which the great crime of our century came to the
birth.

Strange to say, the election of Mr. Lincoln was
hailed with greater joy at the South than at the North.
It was the note of destiny for both, and one at least
understood it. Convinced that cajolery and menace
were henceforth impotent, the South maddened itself
for the assault. Legislatures and conventions plied
their insidious work. The press lit up its baleful fires,
eloquence poured its venomed stream into hearts fevered
by passion, and minds tainted with sophistry and false-
hood; arms threw their angry gleam abroad, and
amid the horrid din, the demon of civil war awoke to
his feast of blood. At the seat of government the
scene was even more disheartening. Imbecility sat
inert in the Presidential chair. Disloyalty plotted in
the bureaus and offices, in the army and navy, in the
highways and byways of the Capital. Traitors legis-
lated in the Congress of the country they had sworn
to destroy. Americans dared to demand a partition of
the soil won by the blood of our common ancestors
And all the while Congress bent its energies to appease,
to soothe, to strengthen the existing guaranties of
slavery, and impart to it new life. And as if all that were
not enough, a peace convention lent its well meant aid,
in proposals which needed but acceptance by the South
to rivet slavery for ever on the land.

It was for such a scene as this that Mr. Lincoln left
his humble home in February, 1861. Since his election
he had kept silence on the questions that agitated the
country, and men waited for his utterances with anxiety.
The wisest of his countrymen did not foresee what the

future had in store. He foresaw, perhaps, less than some of them. But a change had come over him that is well worthy of note. The old faith was doubtless there—the old assurance that the house divided could not stand—that sooner or later the land would be all slave or all free; but there was no longer allusion to it. The leader of a party was now the ruler of a nation, and he felt the full import of the change. Abjuring personal predilections and party views, the safety of the entire nation was henceforth his aim. It became his purpose the instant it became his duty; and until the hour of his death it was the governing principle of his life. Through evil report and good report, in success and disaster, against friends and enemies, he held fast to that; and the hour is already here when we can thank God that he did so. That he thought and felt deeply no one can doubt, but it was with a mind unclouded by prejudgment, and a heart emptied of selfishness.

" My friends," said he, as he parted from that home which he never saw again, " No one not in my position can appreciate the sadness I feel at this parting. I know not how soon I shall see you again. A duty devolves upon me which is, perhaps, greater than that which has devolved upon any other man since the days of Washington. He never would have succeeded except for the aid of Divine Providence, upon which he at all times relied. I feel that I cannot succeed without the same Divine aid which sustained him, and on the same Almighty Being I place my reliance for support; and I hope you, my friends, will all pray that I may receive that Divine assistance, without which I cannot succeed, but with which success is certain."

"We will pray for you," was the feeling response. As we read these words over his grave, who so inert as not to be moved by their solemnity!

All through that journey, whose jubilant life contrasts now so painfully with the return of his funeral train over much of the same ground, this self-restraint and watchfulness,—this reliance on God and reference of all to his direction,—blend themselves with words of wisdom, of caution or remonstrance. "I will only say, that to the salvation of the Union there needs but one single thing,—the hearts of a people like you." And again: "I wish you to remember, now and forever, that it is your business and not mine,"—were his words in Indiana. "I have not maintained silence for want of anxiety. In the varying and repeatedly shifting scenes of the present, and without a precedent that could enable me to judge the past, it has seemed fitting that, before speaking of the difficulties of the country, I should have gained a view of the whole field, so as to be sure after all." Such were his words in Ohio. Here and there touching the sensitive spots of our disorder, he shows his own idea of the malady, but always suggestively. Not concealing entirely his own opinion, he hints it almost always in a query. "Fellow-citizens," he says, "I am not asserting anything; I am merely asking questions for you to consider."

In the metropolis of New York, he speaks somewhat more precisely : "Nothing shall ever bring me to consent—willingly to consent—to the destruction of this Union, unless it would be the thing for which the Union itself was made. I understand that the ship is made for the carrying and preservation of the cargo, and so long as the ship is safe with the cargo, it shall not be aban-

5

doned." And in New Jersey: "The man does not live who is more devoted to peace than I am, or who would do more to preserve it; but it may be necessary to put the foot down firmly."

At that touching scene in the early morning of the 22d of February, when about to raise the country's flag over the birth-place of Independence, he rose to a loftier strain. "I have often inquired of myself," he said, "what great principle or idea it was that kept this confederacy so long together. It was not the mere separation of the colonies from the mother country, but this sentiment in the Declaration of Independence, which gave liberty, not alone to the people of this country, but I hope to the world for all future time. This is the sentiment embodied in the Declaration of Independence. Now, my friends, can this country be saved upon that basis? If it can, I will consider myself one of the happiest men in the world, if I can help to save it. If it cannot be saved upon that principle, it will be truly awful. But if this country cannot be saved without giving up that principle, I was about to say I would rather be assassinated on this spot than surrender,"— and then his sturdy arm sent the colors to the masthead, where God and that arm have kept them since.

A few short years, and he lay a corpse on that very spot, assassinated while defending that very principle; but, thank God, not until it had been triumphantly sustained, and the Union saved upon it.

From the moment when Mr. Lincoln entered upon his duties as President, all narrative is beyond the limits of this discourse. His actions entwined themselves closely with the movements of the nation, themselves various and complicated. He was identified not only in reality, but in the popular apprehension, with all that was done or attempted, great or small. Criticism, favorable or adverse, usually fastened itself in the ultimate upon him, often, undoubtedly, without propriety. But the popular mind continues to recognize certain questions which were treated, during his administration, as of undisputed pre-eminence, and to feel that he held with them a close, and, in effect, controlling relation. His peculiar qualities were displayed in dealing with such, from time to time, and there is a conviction that his reputation will connect itself with them in the future. His relation to some of these may well occupy our remaining time.

Mr. Lincoln was blessed with the faculty, by no means common, of viewing things in their precise and existing relations. He saw things almost always as they really were, and dealt with them as he saw them. However confused the details, his penetration extricated the essential, and his strong good sense and sterling principle applied themselves exclusively to these. Few men have been quicker to see both the weak and the strong point of a position or statement, or more happy in the pointed and simple way in which he exposed and met them.

This sagacity was conspicuous in the attitude which he assumed towards the South at the very outset of his administration. Inexperienced in the details of his new duties; surrounded by friends who knew too little of him to give him their confidence, and too little of the real state of affairs to make their counsel safe; watched by enemies on every hand; beset by spies and the innumerable horde of flatterers and parasites and politicians and self seekers who infest the capital at such

a time; with a powerful voice from the north urging
him to instant and vigorous action, and confusing its
tones with the entreaties of others to pause, beware,
and do nothing; there would have been small room for
wonder if his vision had been obscured and the very
power of action destroyed. But he rose above them all
and surveyed the field for himself.

Rebellion stood quivering upon the brink of the
assault. Ready to strike, it yet longed for some pretext
for the blow,—something that ingenuity might show to
the ignorant world as the justification of its overt act.
A passionate or vain man, a theorist, a partisan,—had
such been at our head,—would probably have sprung
into the melee, drowning the clamor by his own more
decided voice; but it would have been a proof of folly
and not of wisdom. Such a man would have given the
rebellion its desire, and have prejudiced our cause from
the start. But the President perceived the danger and
avoided it. He saw that the war, if it came, must not
only *be*, but record itself as unprovoked. Upon this
idea his inaugural had been constructed. "In your
hands, my dissatisfied fellow-countrymen, not in mine,
is the momentous issue of civil war. The government
will not assail you." "You can have no conflict without being yourselves the aggressors." "We must not
be enemies."

Such were his words, dictated not alone by a kind
spirit, but by a true sagacity. Acting upon them, he
steadily refused to abandon Fort Sumter and thus give
countenance to the rebellion. He was as firm against
the now impracticable work of its reinforcement, so
capable of distortion into an aggressive act. He decided
upon a peaceful attempt to feed its starving garrison.

And this was enough. Sumter fell, but the first gun was a rebel and not a Union gun; and its discharge swept away forever, from the South, the subterfuge of self-defense. Had he done differently, the North would undoubtedly have risen in defense of its outraged flag, but its magnificent unanimity might have been wanting. History must concede it as a high merit to Mr. Lincoln, that, from the outset, he had a purpose, but not a policy; a determinate end, but no predetermined means; a guiding principle, but no controlling rules. In his treatment of the Border States, we can now see the truth and value of this trait. His great object was to strengthen the Union, and weaken the rebellion, and he viewed their position principally as it bore on this. The result we confess to have been of incalculable value, but his course met with little favor, at the time, in any quarter. None saw it aright, until they saw it in its effects. Yet his instructions to a military governor, for a similar scene and at a later day, would seem to show that he measured the crisis very fairly. "If," he writes, "both parties or neither shall abuse you, you will probably be about right. Beware of being praised by one and assailed by the other."

Another conspicuous quality in Mr. Lincoln's character was his power to recognize and appreciate popular opinion. Wise enough to believe, as well as acknowledge, that it was the living principle of every free community, and to confess that neither truth nor error could be permanently affected until brought in direct contact with it; he always bent his energies to discover what that opinion was before he attempted to guide or alter it. The quality was ingrained, and continued to mark him to the last. He looked beneath the apparent

to the real, and distinguished a genuine from a spurious
public sentiment, with skill that seemed intuitive. It
was, however, the product of labor and reflection.
Trusting always to the people, because he felt that
there was nothing higher among men on which to rely,
he often seemed vacillating and uncertain while seeking
what that people really willed. Yet it may be safely
said, that among all his qualities none was more valua-
ble to his countrymen than this. No estimate which he
could have formed, at any time, of the popular feeling
could have long held true, for it was in a course of con-
tinuous growth. With a rare self-abandonment he grew
ever with it. Had he shaped his course by their will,
at any date of his career, and rigidly adhered to it, no
one now so blind as not to see that ruin to him or to
them must have ensued. The country was the people's
more than his. The war was the "people's war;" the
future was the people's destiny and birthright; and he
felt that if the people willed the right, the right, under
God, would triumph, while, for the opposite contingency,
caution preserved his influence unimpaired. Every day
was doing its work of enlightenment upon the popular
mind and heart. Time and experience were potent
and salutary agents. His confidence in them had never
yet been misplaced. He must trust them still.

   This view was the key to his action upon the great
and vexed question of emancipation. His own opinion
of slavery was too clear for misconstruction. It had
been expressed openly and often. "I am naturally
anti-slavery," he writes to a friend in Kentucky. "If
slavery is not wrong, nothing is wrong. I cannot remember the time when I did not so think and feel ; but
I have never understood that the Presidency conferred

upon me an unrestricted right to act officially upon this judgment and feeling." He felt that the Union was to be preserved by that course which would rally about it the most defenders, and leave it, when preserved, what the people willed it. When, at the first, he refused to interfere with slavery as an institution, he was bitterly opposed by many of his friends, but he was right. The time had not come. When he overruled the proclamations of Hunter and Fremont, and the advice of the Secretary of War, to arm the blacks, he taxed the faith of his adherents to its utmost stretch. The indifference and hostility of Europe were, or claimed to be, justified by his course, but he held firm. The time had not come. Personally preferring a compensated emancipation, he suggested it, and devised the means, arguing and expostulating, meanwhile, with the loyal slaveholders, but watching the public will; and when the proclamation came, it is safe to say, that it could no more have been withheld, with safety to the cause, than it could have been issued at an earlier day. The fiery trials of the war had educated the sentiment of the whole people, up to the wishes and judgment of the approving few. Then the time had come. Then it became safe. Then it became his determination, and from that point there was no receding.

A policy of patient watchfulness is seldom grateful to the age to which it may be, nevertheless, essential. The positive, the active, the decided,—these address themselves with favor to the mass of men, while even for the thoughtful they have a charm easily mistaken for a merit. History reverses the hasty decisions of the past, and we adopt her verdict, even while making fresh ones for her disapproval. We confess the indistinctness of our own views and the immaturity of our own opinions, but with a strange confidence we demand their acceptance by our fellow-men. Hesitation in others, we are apt to call weakness; caution, timidity; inquiry, a want of faith; deliberation, cowardice; and the change of actions, to suit the change of circumstance, is dishonesty, if not apostacy. Something of all this may have been permitted by us to tarnish the fame of our noble President, while he lived, but the mark is already obliterated. The tears of the nation have washed it from our sight.

Let us not suppose, my friends, that it cost nothing to Mr. Lincoln to pursue the course which he did; that while waiting for the auspicious hour, he was indifferent to its delay; that the popular desire was his law, but not his solicitude. We should but little sound the depths of that noble nature did we think it. Breathing from his youth the air of perfect freedom, maturing under its gracious influences, drawing his patriotism from the fountain head, and enriching it with the wisdom of the purest American patriots; was his the only cold heart of the race? Dedicated to the faith that slavery is sin, inspired by the conviction that this sin would yet be done away, the moral sting of slavery touched him to the quick. "The physical horrors" he saw, as well as we. The "two hundred and fifty years" of wrong; the "bondman's unrequited toil;" "the drops of blood drawn by the lash;" the scarred limb; the tortured body; the scalding tears,—were felt by him as truly as by us. He could glow at the thought of outraged virtue, of blighted affection, of childhood torn from its parents, of parents from each other. No kindlier heart in all the land responded to their woe. Was he insensible to the plaudits of the good, and did he not well know that the noblest wreath which history twines is for the liberator of mankind? Surely, his eye could range over a more expanded field than ours, and while it saw the coming future, with its hundreds of millions of happy Americans, his ear could catch something of the swelling sounds of praise with which they recognized their great benefactor. Was there no temptation in the sight? Was there nothing within, which could invite,—aye, command to make haste and seize the magnificent prize? Do you think that his hand did not tingle to trace those words which should gleam on the brow of the ages,—the *fiat libertas* of a new creation? Had he no memories of the honored dead,—no inspiring hopes of joining, as an equal, their glorified ranks? Had he not read those words of precious promise,— " Because ye did it to the least of these ye did it unto me?" We may not believe it. Every impulse, every temptation, every implied command which could have addressed itself to any of his countrymen, had a voice for him. But while he heard them, they did not mislead. Behind their lovely and alluring shapes, the Nation reared its austere but hallowed form. " I am your care, and I alone," it said in tones he could not fail to hear. " You and these sufferers are mine." He held his hand. He waited and struggled on. He moved yet awhile in the low grounds of expostulation, but the day at length came when he ascended the height. That glorious proclamation, whose fervid breath melted the fetters from a million limbs, and breathed, " a soul under the ribs of Death," took life at last. His spirit entered its immortal words, and his hand,—the hand that free labor had dignified and

6

formed,—set to its majestic attestation of God and man, the now deathless name of ABRAHAM LINCOLN ! May we not reverently feel that God looked upon all his work, " and it was very good ? "

The most dangerous antagonist with which our peculiar system had to contend, was the fallacy of secession. It was no novelty to Mr. Lincoln, nor had he failed to comprehend it perfectly ; and he perceived at once the advantage of exposing it to the popular eye, in its absurdity as well as its malignity. It was not easy to overturn what the ablest minds of the nation had so carefully established. But in his first message to Congress, at its extra session, he undertook the task. Addressing that body, his arguments and language were brought to the level of his fellow-countrymen, to whom they were really directed. A few vigorous strokes, a few pointed analogies, a short but perfect application of the "*reductio ad absurdum,*" and the creature of perverted ingenuity stood exposed.

" It might seem, at first thought," he says, " to be of little difference whether the present movement at the South be called secession, or rebellion. The movers, however, understand the difference. At the beginning, they knew they could never raise their treason to any respectable magnitude, by any name that implies violation of law."

" They invented an ingenious sophism, which, if conceded, is followed by perfectly logical steps to the complete destruction of the Union."

" With rebellion thus *sugar-coated,* they have been drugging the public mind of their section for more than thirty years."

" The Union is older than the States."

"The States have their status *in the Union*, and they have no other legal status."

"No one of them ever had a State constitution, independent of the Union."

"A power to destroy the government itself has never been known as a governmental power."

"These politicians are not partial to that power which made the Constitution, and speaks from the Preamble, calling itself, 'We, the People.'"

"The central idea of secession is the essence of anarchy."

Such are but a few of the home thrusts which he dealt, every one of which, an average American could comprehend and feel. The intellects of a Marshall, a Story and a Webster have exercised themselves with triumph upon the same theme, but the quaint words of this unlettered Western lawyer, produced an effect greater than they all.

There is no principle,—and there should be none,—dearer to a free people than that of their personal liberty. Freemen, in all times, have clung to it as a right too sacred to be limited in terms; and those time-honored words, "*habeas corpus*," which, to the popular mind, stand its all-powerful guardians, have acquired for them a consecrated, but undefined meaning. The exigencies of our conflict brought Mr. Lincoln into collision with this sentiment, though, perhaps, never with the right; and few measures of his administration have subjected him to a fiercer onslaught than his suspension of that writ. Whether his view of the constitution, as designating the department which should exercise the power, in a given case, was right or wrong, is a point upon which able men still differ. That the right to exercise

it existed, none disputed at the time. That it was
necessary to exercise it, few, at this day, dispute. That
no injury to the liberties of the people was designed, is
universally allowed. That none has resulted is patent
to all. If the candid criticism of the future shall find
that Mr. Lincoln erred, it will probably be in his opinion, that the power could be delegated by him. But
this, if an error, he himself corrected; and throughout
his whole course, he ever referred his conduct to Congress, and received its support and endorsement. He
held to the axiom that " The public safety is the highest
law; " he knew that public liberty demands, at times,
the subordination of private liberty, and with what
adroitness and point did he popularize the idea.

"I can no more be persuaded that the Government
can constitutionally take no strong measures in time of
rebellion, because it can be shown that the same could
not be lawfully taken in time of peace, than I can be
persuaded that a particular drug is not good medicine
for a sick man, because it can be shown not to be good
food for a well one." And again : when alluding to the
supposed risk that the public would acquire a relish for
arbitrary power, dangerous to its liberties, he doubts
that "a man could contract so strong an appetite for
emetics, during temporary illness, as to persist in feed-
ing on them during the remainder of his healthful life."
There are more elegant figures, and there are weaker.

Without a trace of that personal ambition which can
trample on liberty while claiming to defend it; without
a single feeling of hostility to even the bitterest oppo-
nent; with a calm temper, which knew not the meaning of revenge; with a cool courage that never magni-
fied dangers, and an habitual self-control, which gave

an air almost of hesitancy to his conduct,—his would
have been the last hand to deal a blow, whether open
or covert, at the liberties of the humblest of the race.
It was because he died for those liberties that you weep
him now.

While dealing prominently with the active principles
of the rebellion, it should not be imagined that the
President overlooked any of the great national interests
confided to him. The financial, industrial, and, especially, the agricultural prospects of the country, were
objects of his constant care, and of frequent and judi-
cious recommendations. In all the departments of
government, he had the aid of zealous and able men,—
men whom the country will ever delight to honor with
her grateful praise; but it belongs to his own credit, that,
while they all received his confidence and a chivalrous
support, not one of them was ever able to assume a
control over his intelligence or conduct, which could
prejudice the one, or disparage the other. If we would
estimate this as we should, we need not look to the
Buckinghams and Butes, the Mazarins or Godoys, of
former times, or the Antonellis and DeMornys, of to-
day; the short line of our own governmental history
will—

"Give ample room and verge enough,
The character to trace."

Towards foreign countries, Mr. Lincoln preserved a
deportment of which Americans may be proud, and for
which they can never be too grateful; for he defended
their true interests and dignity against the pleadings
of their own high spirit, the sting of unprovoked hostility, and the languor of drooping patriotism. Ameri-

can in every fibre of his nature, he felt that if Liberty
triumphed, it must be by the hands of her own children,
and that those hands must be held from even defensive
wrong. It was a perilous course through which he had
to guide. The single rib of steel which spanned Pada-
lon's gulf was scarcely narrower, or reared over greater
dangers, but he sat unmoved:

> " Steady and swift the self-moved chariot went,
>   Winning the long ascent,
>   Then downward rolling, gains the farther shore."

We must have moulted our memories, as the birds their
last year's feathers, if we have forgotten the perils of
the way. But the firmness of Lincoln and the genius
of Seward bore us through.

While the country was rejoicing over the captured
rebel emissaries in the Trent, and England refusing to
await an explanation, brandished her club in our faces,
and threatened us with war, it was not an easy task to
say to a high spirited people, " We have erred; we
must retrace our steps." Yet, he said it, and in such a
way that malice itself could not misinterpret the motive.
A world in arms could not move us from the right.
Our dignity withdrew us from the wrong. When that
same England, false to the accredited spirit of her stock,
was warm to the enemies of liberty, and icy to its friends;
when her leading journal poured out daily its taunts
and glad predictions of defeat, taxing its ingenuity to
malign our motives and falsify our achievements,—to
encourage our enemies and intimidate our friends,—to
destroy our credit, and grow rich by our sufferings;
when the pirates that preyed upon our commerce issued

from her ports, completely fitted for their work, and
returned from their dastardly rapine, to be applauded, .
and to refit ; when every colony she owned was practi-
cally shut to us, and open to our foes; and Canada,
Australia, the Cape and the Atlantic Islands vied with
each other for her approval, by insult and outrage of
every sort,—it would not have been difficult to unite
the people in a declaration of just and deadly war. But
it might have been our ruin. When France, emboldened
by our trials, advanced the banner of her Latin civilization, and defied the sentiment of our race by the conquest of Mexico, there were a provocation and a danger
of the greatest magnitude ; but our path was carried
clear of both. Nor were the peoples of the world, at
any moment, in doubt of what we meant or what we
were about. Aristocracy and Despotism painted the
picture as they wished it, but the common people removed the obscuring pigment, by the alchemy of a
common interest and a common aspiration, and read
the outline as it was. They felt for us, for they hoped
to enjoy with us; and the messages of cheer which they
sent to us across the water abide in our hearts. Popular sympathy Mr. Lincoln recognized with delight.
Foreign insult and hostility he noted ; but, for the time,
he passed them by. Foreign intervention he indig-
nantly repudiated from the first. The value of this
service, time will reveal.

A close and thorough scrutiny of Mr. Lincoln's acts
and words will not fail to show him, to all coming time,
as one of the great men of the world—one of those be-
ings upon whom the sacred seals were set, " That give
the world assurance of a man." Great in his intellectual
composition for the uses and the audience to which his

mind was called to address itself, he was even greater
in the moral. The action of his mind was easy, vigorous and remarkably direct. Always starting from
principles, a true and even subtle logic bore him to his
conclusions without divergence. If he disclosed the
processes, it was in a phraseology altogether distinctive
of the man, and which brought him close to the hearts
and intelligence of those whom he addressed, while a
play of homely humor, and touches of descriptive anec-
dote and illustration, brightened and deepened the im-
pression. Strong common sense dominated over all,
but it mated with the keenest subtlety of thought, and
only prescribed the dress of a most natural and fitting
phrase. He was no scholar, in the technical sense,—no
orator, beyond a limited range. For the flights of im-
passioned oratory, his emotional nature was too sluggish,
or too carefully repressed; but in tenderness and pathos,
he felt his way to the heart with a success that genius
might envy. In his letters and speeches we see no
striving after effect for effect's sake. It was not in his
nature. No man ever rose to power in our country who
was so truly a representative American as he. Foreign
travel, an acquaintance with foreign languages and
manners, intercourse with the distinguished men of other
lands, one or the other, had exercised an influence upon
most of our public men; but he was absolutely unaf-
fected by any. Society had not rubbed down the outline of his character to fit its own conventional mould.
His heart, his hopes, his tastes, his pursuits, his affections,
and, perhaps, his prejudices, had been those of the mass
of his fellow countrymen. His reasoning was adapting
itself to their minds while it was shaping itself in his
own. His imagery kept company with theirs. His

illustrations never outreached their memory and fancy.
His wit and humor had a home tone to their ears. He
allowed them to see into him at all times, and they
recognized a man in substance like themselves. He
had met and conquered difficulties as they had done,
and they saw, in his grapple with new ones, the sort of
struggle they would have wished to put forth themselves. He was a true man of the people, in the struc-
ture both of body and of mind.

But it was his moral nature that was his crown of
glory and of strength. Temperament undoubtedly did
much for him. It did much for his cheerfulness, his
tenderness of heart, his unruffled and most blessed
temper; but it could not have done all. There was a
deeper spring that fed the benignity which knew no
bitterness to anybody, even to traitors and foes; which
repressed them as divine justice would dictate, in a spirit
of love to what is right, and of uncompromising opposition to the wrong, with a view to repentance and
return. A mind perfectly self-sustained, because sustained by a principle of duty referred always to the will
and word of God, was his foundation stone, and it was
laid by the One who alone can lay it. That neither
anger, nor envy, nor pride, nor petulance, nor disap-
pointment,—that no misapplied virtue, nor any vice, that
simulated virtue,—ever moved it from its settled base
was the labor, and is now the honor of his life. Whatever he was, too, he was, in the midst of myriad embar-
rassments and novelties; of trying disasters, alternating
with as trying success; of incessant labor, watchfulness
and weariness; of factious opposition, and as factious
support; of misrepresentation and misconstruction; and

7

yet without yielding, in a single instance, to anger, or even to irritation.

A certain external dignity might have made his office seem higher, without being so in the least, but the assumption of it, in his ordinary carriage, would have marred the pleasant picture he has left. We should not have seen him as he truly was, accessible and equable to all, because kind, humane and excellent at heart. We could not have looked within his breast, as he so often let us do, and taken comfort for our own in the gloomy days. It is true that the noble sentences of his inaugurals, and messages, and proclamations; the tender sublimity of his Gettysburg oration, which will live while the language lives; the inspiring and prophetic utterances of his later days,—these would still have remained, and we might well thank God for the precious gift. But the man of our love and admiration, we should have missed.

He who fails to feel that God's hand has been over us in the progress of our struggle, may also fail to see that His was the selection of the man who led us. He gave us the man for our wants, and left us to discover in him the man of our desires. The nation needed him, but it did not choose him, at first, from any perception of its need. It looked for a ruler, but it got far more. If we test his administration by its principles, it was upright; if by its results, it was eminently successful; if by its influences, it was elevating. Yet it was an administration which found us united upon its merits only at its close. Then his true value stood revealed; and then, a grateful people paid its tribute of approbation by electing him its ruler for a second term.

It was well said of Washington, that " he changed

mankind's ideas of political greatness." And it might be said, with equal truth, of Abraham Lincoln. He carried still further the change which that venerated man began, and lifted the judgments of mankind to a higher level. Yet, what greatness and power does not that praise assert. Is it so small a work? While a Cæsar, a Bonaparte, a Cromwell, and a Washington alike receive our praise, can it be said that we have yet learned what real political greatness is? We are, however, learning it; and that we are, is in large measure, the work of him who has gone. God has set the seal of success to principles and practices which, henceforth, we may not dare to underrate. The man of the people has taught the people how to estimate themselves and him. He has lifted for their admiration, truth and candor, simplicity and charity, the graces of soul before the accomplishments of mind; and has drawn them back through the luminous pathway of those virtues to the eternal principles which glorify them all. He purged our vision until the eye, which even brilliant vice could once dazzle, can now look into the pure, bright light of virtue, and grow stronger. And this he has done. not amid the tranquillity of peace, but the fire and blood of a fearful civil war. Great armies swept over the land. Great navies scourged the sea. The energies of a gigantic race strained in the conflict. It gave its treasure, its valor, its skill,—and he directed all. It was repulsed, and he encouraged and planned anew. It was victorious, and he applauded. It conquered, and he secured the conquest. It suffered, and he pitied and consoled. It wept its dead, and he wept them with it. It praised him, and he turned its praises to themselves,— to the soldier, the sailor, the toiling mother, the self-sacrificing wife, the steadfast living, the honorable dead. It abused him, and he was silent; but heart, and hand, and head kept on their fearless and protective work.

And what results for the future was he not preparing? He was liberating the intellect as well as the bodies of a race. He was making the freedom of the world,—of all men in all climes,—henceforth a certainty. He was dissolving the bonds between the falsehoods and iniquities of the old and new worlds. He was teaching a lesson to tyrants and emancipators alike. Commanding armies such as the world never saw before, he was binding all their glories to the cause of civil liberty. Controlling treasure almost boundless, he was uncorrupted and uncorrupting.

While we reflect upon this, and while our grief takes fresh bitterness from the thought of what he might have continued to be to us, let us not overlook the glory with which a gracious God vouchsafed to crown his many excellencies during his life,—the glory that our eyes have already seen. His administration "was sown in weakness, but it was raised in power." It began in whispering fear; it ended in exulting pæans. Yet its weakness was even, at first, more apparent than real. Behind him was the exhaustless strength of the North and West. At his side, and waiting for his word, were those brave and able men, like him self-dedicated to their country,—that illustrious band,—the wreaths for whose living brows, and the chaplets for whose dead, the Nation alone must weave. Victors and martyrs for the Union, no State can henceforth single out her own, but each shall find its representative in all. Those majestic words of the latest Hebrew prophet seem to come to me with a meaning for these times: "Prove

me now, saith the Lord of Hosts, if I will not open you
the windows of Heaven, and pour you out a blessing
that there shall not be room enough to receive it."
They proved him with the costliest offering,—the offering of self,—and the blessing came. Port Royal, and
Hatteras, and Newbern, and Roanoke, and New Orleans,
Columbus and Island No. 10, and Vicksburg, and Knox-
ville, and Chattanooga, and Atlanta, and Savannah, and
Charleston, and Richmond. These are the gems which
heaven-sent Victory dropped from her tiara as she
moved across the continent. Clinging forever to our
now consecrated flag, they shall shine along its stripes,
and give new brightness to its undiminished stars. He
saw them set in its glorious field and gleaming in its
folds. Victory paused before his eye, and waved her
broad wings over all the land, in tremulous benediction.
The flag of Sumter was restored while he lived. The
foundation army of the rebellion surrendered to the
army of which he was Commander-in-chief. His own
foot had trod the capital of treason, and his own ear
had heard the simple blessings of the race which God,
through him, had freed. On land and on sea the Union
was triumphant, and to his vision peace and prosperity
were already near. It was a closer view than that from
Pisgah's top, and a grander. God, in mercy, permitted
it to the eye which was so soon to close in death, and
his own tongue has confessed its blessedness and peace.
 "*Vero felix non vitæ tantum claritate sed etiam oppor-
tunitate mortis.*"
 But the end was at hand. At the very moment
when all is joy and exultation,—when the hearts of all
beat strong, and the nation stretches out its hand to the
repentant and returning,—the demon of Slavery strikes

its expiring blow. With hell in his heart and fustian on his lips, the ruffian representative of this hideous iniquity springs upon the scene, and fires the fatal shot which opens for Abraham Lincoln the abodes of enduring blessedness; for himself, the caverns of despair.

How terrible the blow! How awful the shock! Faith alone remains unparalysed; but is not faith our vital principle? Is not faith his best memorial?

My fellow-citizens, is it the death of a man that we lament, or the sin of a man that we condemn? It seems to me that we shall perceive but little of the awful truth, if we think so. Southern secession, Southern barbarism, but, first of all, Southern slavery,—and Northern sympathy with all or any of them,—these are the felons for our judgment; the spirit of liberty and law, the destiny of man, and the will of God,—these are what were assailed. These clothed themselves in the forms of the noble victim, and of his ignoble assassin. High bred men, and delicate women, who have not blushed to praise and cherish this malignant institution,—who have rated its merchandise as of more worth than family purity, and national life, and human progress,—may startle at the thought, that in their souls could lurk one seed of that which flowered in assassination. But let them look more closely. Even in that cultured soil may have been the rootlets of this poison-plant. The crime of murder lay folded in the crime of slavery, and he who cherished the one has, unknowingly it may be, reared the other. The picture is even more appalling so, but we must not shut our eyes. We owe it to the destinies of our race; we owe it to the character and memory of the dead; we owe it to our own moral sense, if we would not see it palsied forever ; we owe it to the majesty of the law for which so many of our brethren have fought, and starved, and died,—to look through the agents in this crime, to its guiltier principal ; and to let righteousness be the plummet of our judgment.

Let us not be too solicitous about the law, and its retributions. Let us not strive to influence the utterances of that majestic spirit, " whose seat," we say, " is the bosom of God, her voice the harmony of the world." Her judgments and her sentences will be carried out only so far as the public sentiment permit. Let us rather clarify the portion which we ourselves contribute to that sentiment. Let us see to it, that in our minds, treason is not suffered to be the synonym for heroism in defence ; nor rebellion, for difference in political opinion ; nor slavery for anything but sin. Let us see that justice is meted, in our own estimates and opinions, to the high as well as to the low,—the justice of disapproval, of degradation, of infamy, if such be called for ; and let it settle on the leaders and the gentlemen of crime, and on them most heavily ; or else, let us hide our faces before the prisoned thief, and sentenced murderer. Let us set up the true standard within our souls, and then " *with malice towards none, with charity for all, with firmness in the right as God gives us to see the right, let us strive on to finish the work we are in.*"

" He mourns the Dead who lives as they desire," is truth, in poetry.

This mighty nation has mourned the illustrious dead with the full outpourings of spontaneous sorrow. The tones of its lamentation have reached across the earth, and have waked responsive echoes from its farthest borders. Never, since Creation's dawn, did such universal grief attend the death of one man. None could indifferently observe where all were mourners. We still regard the sublime scene with awe. But our mourning cannot end here. In the imperfect sketch which I have presented of this great and good man, I have failed entirely, if I have left it necessary still to point out the virtues which invite the imitation of our people. We find them in his life. Let us then live as he lived—as he would have had us live. With God's will for our guide, and our country's welfare our aim, let the virtues of our beloved President be the pilots and attendants of our course. Let our patriotism be not so much that which asserts, as that which demonstrates itself. Let our courage be not that which defies, but that which sustains and disarms opposition. Let our constancy be not the parasite of prosperity, but the living outgrowth of deep rooted faith. Let our firmness be not that of the rock which repels, but rather, that of the sturdy pine, which bends responsive to the varying breezes which move but cannot overturn it. Let us believe less in what men style the destiny of nations, of races, of men ; and more in the destiny of principles and truths. Let us move in that path which the beams of conscience and reason may combine to illumine, and so move, as men who acknowledge that the greatness of their nation and its liberties are a sacred trust committed to them for the welfare of mankind. Let the American nation lay deep the solid corner stone of right, and upon that foundation let it rear to the memory of Abraham Lincoln the noblest monument it can—the monument of an imitated example.

Illum, "*admiratione potius quam temporalibus laudibus, et si natura suppeditet, etiam æmulatione decoremus.*"